D0435943

{GOD'S} BLOGS

INSIGHTS FROM HIS SIGHT

lanny donoho

Multnomah® Publishers *Sisters, Oregon*

GOD'S BLOGS
published by Multnomah Publishers, Inc.
(These are good people.)
© 2005 by Lanny Donoho
Author created by God with help from Orville and Clara Donoho in 1953

International Standard Book Number: 1-59052-535-3
Basketball jersey number in high school: 22

Scripture quotations are from:
The Holy Bible, New International Version
©1973, 1984 by International Bible Society,
used by permission of Zondervan Publishing House
New American Standard Bible © 1960, 1977, 1995
by the Lockman Foundation. Used by permission.
The country song referenced on pp. 200–201 is "Live Like You Were Dying"
by Tim McGraw.

Multnomah is a trademark of Multnomah Publishers, Inc.,
and is registered in the U.S. Patent and Trademark Office.
The colophon is a trademark of Multnomah Publishers, Inc.
Printed in the United States of America

For information:
MULTNOMAH PUBLISHERS, INC.
POST OFFICE BOX 1720
SISTERS, OREGON 97759
(OH, BROTHER)
05 06 07 08 09 10—10 9 8 7 6 5 4 3 2 1

Dedication

To Orville and Clara Donoho,

Dad and Mom.

Dad showed me truth.

Mom was faith in the flesh,

when faith was really hard.

Nondisclaimer

In case there are those out there who would have a problem
with someone writing or speaking for God…

Try to relax.

This book is supposed to be an *enjoyable look at the principles God* put in the Bible…and they're done with a twist.

For some people it is easier to grasp the grace and truth of
God if they feel like His word is personal to them…from
Him.

Everybody has their ideas of what God might want to say to them.

These are mine.

{GOD'S BLOGS}

All bloggers have

their own profile.

This is mine.

Things I created that I really like:

WIND...
the way it blows in tornadoes...the gentleness
of it softly brushing against the grains in a field of
wheat.

Eyes
(how they speak more clearly than mouths)

SMILES

WATER...
all of its forms...
falls, rain, icicles, rivers, lakes, *tears*.

Light...
its speed and form.
How it helps you see.
How it sprinkles the night just right.

Colors
The BRAIN...
I like that every single one
is different and that each of them
continue to change each second.

**Oh...and I really like how I made you.
You are different and wonderfully
unique, and I created you that way in
your mother's belly. I consider each of
you My masterpiece.**

The platypus makes ME smile.

**And then the things I made
that thrill you and Me both...**

Music

LAUGHTER

Friendship

Taste buds

What happens in the soul
when lovers touch

Names humans call Me:

Yahweh

Creator

Alpha

Omega

I Am

Abba ← My favorite. It means. <u>Daddy</u> for those of you who havent studied other languages

Favorite stuff I have done:

Setting the universe up to spin like it does…
like a giant mobile.

That Red Sea incident.

Surprise Lazarus! You're *back!*

The whole Jonah episode.

Used people no one knows
to make a difference in millions of lives.

Sent Jesus to the earth!

Rolled away that stone so He could come out and
show you who I really AM.

Created YOU in MY image. (You look good.)

You'll hear about more in the blogs.

Contact Info.

Just call Me…

out **loud,**

in your head,

with your *heart.*

I'll get it.

The blog before the blogs

Since there are millions of humans blogging all the time and other millions reading those millions, I thought I'd get in on the act and see who might be interested in My day-to-day random entries. One problem I have is that here I AM outside of time, and these web pages automatically put a date on the entry. I could override that—I AM God. But I think you readers are sharp enough to know that if I said "Today I surprised Moses and made a bush burn in front of him without burning up," the day I'M talking about would be a long time ago to you…even though the entry might read August 21, 2005. Part of the problem I have with communicating with humans is this whole "time" thing. Today I AM chatting with Moses and today I AM speaking to James McDaniel who was born in 2021 and is praying for his mother right now.

That's why I called Myself I AM. I was even watching some of you read this…before it was typed.

I know that whole concept throws some of you off balance. If you need to feel more comfortable, just imagine you are in a Hitchcock movie, *The Twilight Zone, The Matrix,* or maybe even *Shadows in Time.* (If you're reading this before the year 2008, then you don't know of that last film yet.)

The fact is, I started and finished all of these blogs before the word *blog* existed. I just had to wait till you had the word and the concept before I put them in the brain of someone in your century and had him put them into words.

Basically I'M entering into your blogdom because *somehow the rumor got started that I was kind of **boring.***

For those of you who bought into that craziness, you should know that I'M the one who created all the stuff you love…all the stuff that makes life exciting.

I invented *funny*.

and **LAUGHTER**.

I created **ADVENTURE**
and *Romance*.

I even came up with the concept of
c o m m u n i c a t i o n .

I can communicate across the world in nanoseconds
(without intel inside).

I know your soul,

and what makes you happy

and sad.

So, I plan on dispelling some of the misconceptions about who I AM...and painting a new picture of Me...just for you. And maybe I'll paint a new picture of you...(one that you haven't seen before).

Some of My blogs will make some of you laugh, and others of you will think I'M weird.

I AM. *Hey! That last phrase was both a statement AND My name*

Some of you laughed at that. Some of you would laugh if I said you had to get the blog out of your own eye before you can remove the spec from someone else's. Some of you have no idea what I'M talking about.

I'll use a human to write these.

Of course, using a human means he might misinterpret some of My thoughts or use some of his own to say what he thinks I AM thinking, but it'll be a fun thing watching people read and respond. The particular human I AM using for this one is a bit different than most. He'll probably get some strange artist to doodle *a doodle* on the pages and put photographs in the middle of blogs that don't seem to make any sense.

I'M sure he will play around with different **FONTS** and he will use ellipses way too much…

Anyway…

Who knows (I mean, besides Me)?

I might even put it into a publisher's head to make this into a book.

I just want to let you know what some of My thoughts and hopes for you are.

I already put a lot of that in My bestseller (sixty-six books in one). I continue to speak through lots of people and circumstances, but this will be a unique way to show some who think I'M old and outdated that I AM still relevant.

Because…   hey…

I'M a blogger.

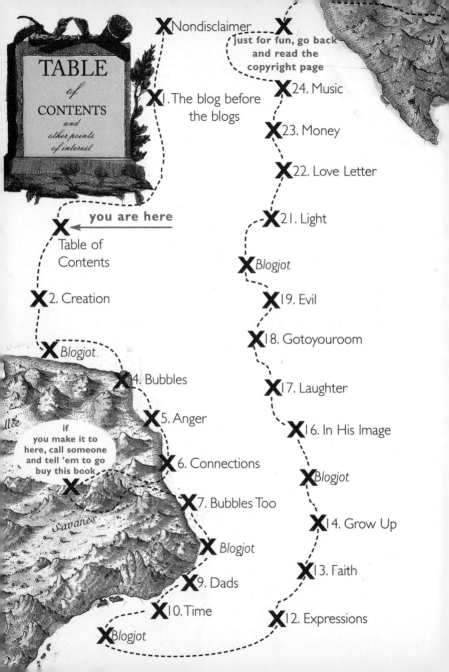

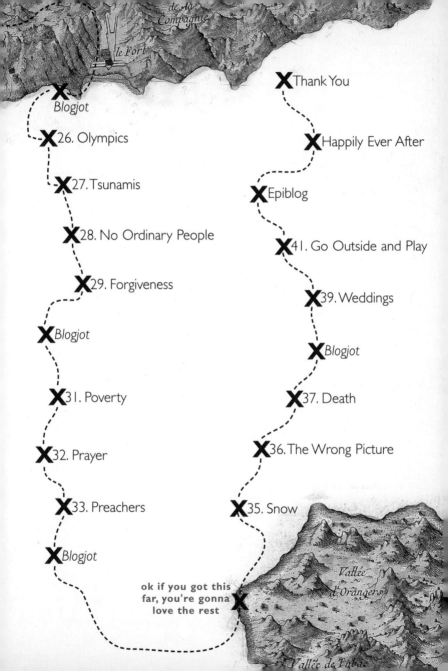

2. CREATION

Wow! I really started something this week.

I created a universe.

Yep, a whole universe with stars and planets,

galaxies

and big  black holes,

lots of movable parts and colors and

everything.

It's pretty cool.

I got a little bit carried away. I started with just little pieces: atoms or smaller protons and electrons. Most of you know about those. Some of you even know about the smaller pieces called neutrinos and quarks and subquarks. There are even smaller pieces…but you haven't found them…<u>yet.</u> You will…and you'll be <u>amazed!</u>

Anyway, I took these tiny little pieces and formed space and moons and solar systems and some things that you can't imagine but are bigger than anything you can get your head around.

I focused a lot of My attention on this one ball of dirt and water.

I made living creatures, the sky, clouds, grass, trees, oceans, elephants, whales, insects, amoebas, slugs, frogs, hippos, kangaroos, pandas, opossums, skunks, and the list goes on and on. ⌐ that was fun

Sorry for the long list…I get carried away every time I think of it. It was just a great fun week.

Then toward the end of the week...I made My most astounding creation. It's amazing what God can do when He mixes some dirt and water and cells and then breathes some God-life into it.

It's the closest thing to

ME

I've ever created.

When My first human opened his eyes and took his

first breath, we just stared at each other in the face.

Then I started laughing,

and he didn't know what to do
(mainly because he had never done anything before).

But as he looked at Me and saw Me smiling…

it was just natural for him to smile back

(that's the way I made him).

I was so **excited** and **elated** and **laughing** all over!

For a while all I could do was just watch him.

Then we talked…and new synapses formed in his brain

(just like I made them to) and he learned…and we

both had experiences that had never existed

before…even for Me.

It was great, but the whole time,

I knew something was missing.

He felt it too.

What happened next almost made

Me surprise Myself! I took part of

that man and formed something...

some ONE...that made both of us

step back in wonder.

When the man stepped back, he almost fell into a canyon.

When I stepped back, I almost fell off the edge of eternity (metaphorically speaking).

SHE WAS INCREDIBLE!

I laughed again, and then I cried. The man did the same thing I did; (he's a lot like Me).

He needed a word that wasn't there yet.

I gave it to him:

≥Thanks≤

We'd never had gratitude before.

It was exactly as I'd hoped it would be.

I said, "You're welcome," and then I stepped away for a while so he could bask…and I could be alone again.

Interesting feelings for Me: much joy…huge elation about what I had just created…

but I wanted to be able to _not_ know what was getting

ready to happen.

Like I said, I really started something this week.

And even though I know everything that's about to

happen, I'd still have to say…

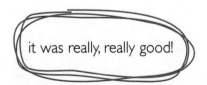

it was really, really good!

Blogjot

I broke one of the blog rules by putting

Mine in a book.

A blog is a web log.

That is where it gets its name.

So the blogs in this book really aren't blogs

because they aren't on the Web.

Maybe they should be called **KLOGS**.

4. BUBBLES

July 17, 2006

A lot of the stuff I've created is fairly complex:

the Northern Lights

the mysterious-but-miraculous human brain

how the moon and gravity affect the tides

One of my more brilliant children understood quantum physics to a certain degree and how time and space related to one another, but he had a really hard time with quantum mechanics and how it could be that masses on the subatomic level didn't seem to act the same as the larger masses in space.

MYSTERY IS GOOD.

It keeps people searching.

And periodically – when they discover something they didn't understand before – they get to see a little more of what I AM like.

I like watching brilliant minds try to unravel the mystery…but I also love watching people mesmerized by the simple treasures of life.

Some of the most simple things often reveal my desire for splendor in your lives.

Today I watched a young man playing with bubbles.

He was actually 45 years old…which seems young to ME but old to some of you. His wife and children were gone, and he was washing the dishes. A soap bubble (seemingly by happenstance) formed on the edge of the sink and rose into the air. He turned and looked, and his mind raced back to when he was a kid. Realizing he was alone and wanting to feel this feeling from his past for a bit longer, he reached under the sink and pulled out the dishwashing soap and poured it into the water. He found the right utensils in the drawer and dipped one into the soapy water, lifted it…and blew.

Not enough soap. He poured in more. He mixed it well. He dipped in the utensil, lifted it…and blew again. Out came a bubble the size of a baseball.

A different utensil, a little more soap, another blow, and there floating in front of him was a bubble the size of a softball.

Another try and there was one the size of his Uncle Leroy's head.

I made that head knew it was going to end up being a size 8 before he was even born

He watched these bubbles –

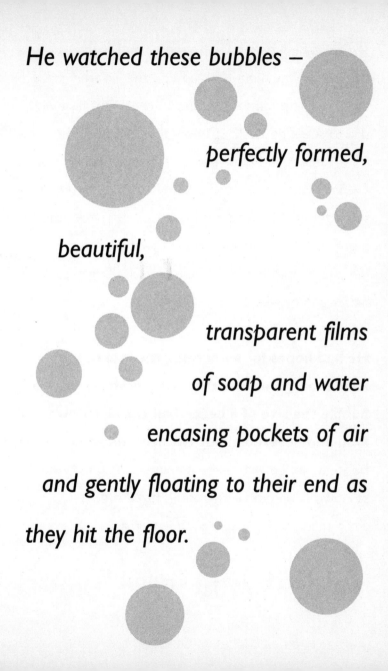

perfectly formed,

beautiful,

transparent films

of soap and water

encasing pockets of air

and gently floating to their end as

they hit the floor.

At times he would take the utensil and try to catch them and blow them back up into the air again just to make them last longer (and to check out his own skill to see if he could still hold the record of the most catches and blow-backs he had held back in 1965). It was almost time for the family to be home, so he thought he would try one more thing. A little more soap, a careful dip…a very gentle but forceful blow. Out from the end of the utensil it began to be bigger and bigger.

He had hopes for something the size of the Hindenburg but was absolutely ecstatic when a bubble the size of a beach ball closed its own loop and hovered about two feet above his head. It swirled with rainbow colors and drifted ever so slowly toward his living room. He followed it in amazement. In his mind, it was the ultimate.

It was perfect!

It wobbled and drifted, and he watched,

holding his breath,

hoping that he could enjoy his creation as long as possible.

He didn't want it to land.

And it didn't. The front door of his house opened and his seven-year-old son came bounding in and immediately saw the bubble and shouted,

"Wow, Dad, that's cool!"

And then without thinking he just destroyed it.

He took his hand and purposefully punctured that thin layer of film holding that air. *No, he purposefully took his hand and punctured that beautiful and wonderful perfect creation of his dad's.*

And it was still four feet from the ground.

Dad never got to watch and enjoy his perfect creation naturally and beautifully float to its expected destination.

He knew it was silly to feel the way he did because the bubble wasn't going to last anyway…but it was his creation…and it was incredible…and he wanted to watch it all the way to the ground. He knew he couldn't be angry with his son because his son couldn't understand. Kids think that's what you do with bubbles. So he chose not to be mad. As a matter of fact he reached down and hugged his son and told him *he loved him*. He turned around and went back to the kitchen and sadly stood quietly over the dirty dishwater.

…his thoughts turned to me…
and my creation …
and my elation…
and my disappointment…
and my love…

... and the man smiled.

5. ANGER

[Ya can't always get what ya want.]

You all know people who struggle because they have problems now and then controlling their ANGER.

Most of you know what it feels like for anger to grab hold of your soul and take control, even when you don't want it to.

Since I created anger and meant for it to be a part of your life, it does have its place. However, My intent was for anger to motivate you so that when you saw things that were wrong, you would do what was in your power to make them right. This doesn't mean to lash out when you feel you personally have been wronged. Anger was placed inside your genes to help change things that you know I want changed.

It is kinda like pain. I created pain in your body to alert you when something is wrong with your system and so you can do something about it. Your anger response is part of your genetic makeup for basically the same reason. When you are aware that something is wrong with the system I created (people are getting hurt; they are starving or dying for reasons of neglect or selfishness; people or institutions are doing things that misrepresent Me), then anger helps you to do something about it. I must say that you've drifted a long way from that perspective.

Think about this. Anger happens within most of you most of the time for one simple reason. **You don't get what you want.**

— It's pretty much that simple. —

You want something and you can't have it so you get angry and your anger controls you and consequently people get hurt. *including yourself*

But—I'M sure you've noticed—this kind of anger results in yelling, screaming, arguing, hitting, hurting, stress, depression, revenge, drug use, relational disorders, and more physiological and psychological disturbances than any of you even know of yet.

It messes things up on the cellular level that escalate to a universal level that can last for generations.

All because you want something and you just can't have it.

Step back, and see the larger picture:

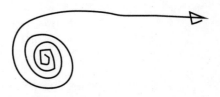

I created you.

I love you more than you love yourself.

I want the very best for you,

and

I know all your needs and everything it takes

to make your life as fulfilled

as it can possibly be.

If there is something you want and you
don't get it…the chances are extremely
high that you don't really want it.

Why?

Because you want the best thing for you, and you don't know all the time what that is.

You can't see the big picture.

But hey! I do.

For example, if you don't have it, that probably means I don't think you're supposed to yet. Or ever.

Which would mean whatever it is you want that you don't have—if you got it, your life would be not as full (emptier).

Are you following this?

Get to know Me. When you get to know Me, you will begin to know better My thoughts and My desires for you. And you will learn to trust Me. And then when your human hearts says, "I want that!" there will be a part of you that says, "only if You want it for me, God."

And when your heart gets to that point, anger subsides.

(I created a thing called patience that grows in you when you grow in Me.)

And when your heart gets better, so does the rest of your body and all your relationships, and then, all of a sudden, you **live longer** and **love more**…and all the things you really want become yours.

That's what I meant when I said "by losing your life, you find it" and by "loving your life, you lose it."

Okay, I know there are a lot of you who actually are consumed, and it doesn't help a lot to hear somebody say "**chill out**"…which is how I thought about ending this.

I know you can't just decide to chill out.

And it takes a while for a personality to change.

So take some time. Process.

Next time you feel yourself tighten up, and you know your face is red, and you're ready to yell or lash out, and you know that your anger is just about to take over, think about what it is that you want that you can't have (the thing that is making you angry).

Then try to remember.

The only way to really get what you want is to give it up.

Then you'll get what you really want…way down in the depths of your soul.

One more thing. I'M here for ya.

Hang with Me for a while.

Get to know Me. Learn to trust Me.

Then you'll know what I want

and you'll want what I want.

And what I want is for some of your wants to change…

and if they do…

we'll all get what we want.

Have a nice day.

6. CONNECTIONS

Today I listened to millions of prayers. Many of them were from hurting people begging Me for intervention and asking Me *why*.

In order for you to understand, I'll use the human vernacular for just a second and say that My heart aches for you so often.

I see and feel your pain and do what I know is best…and yet, I know

<u>you cannot understand for now.</u>

There is a concept you can understand though, and if you grab hold of it, it might help.

It's about your connections.

Many of you are unaware of your role in the universe and how important your every thought and word and deed are.

They are connected to others in ways

you will never see.

A thread makes its way through history, and you are tied to it.

People are put into your path. It is important that you notice them and that you talk to Me about them, *and especially that you hear from Me on how to act and react to them.*

Let Me tell you about a family that I see right now.

In a crib in Phoenix, Arizona, lies a little infant named Megan.

Megan was born a few months ago with a birth defect.

Her mother is sitting in a rocking chair in the living room of their little house praying to Me.

She is also feeling somewhat guilty that her child was born like this.

Let Me tell you what I see in the future of that little girl.

Her mother realizes she can't bear this burden alone, and she begins to rely on Me to help her.

Little Megan grows up surrounded by love. She hears her mother tell her Bible stories and stories about Me and My love. She attends a church where in spite of her "not being normal," she is loved by a youth group. I watch as she learns and grows and loves.

I watch her at her wedding where over three hundred people weep and smile and hardly notice any unnatural deformities because they are so mesmerized by her countenance.

Their smiles are there because they know her heart. Her life has given them encouragement.

Megan's mom has given them a gift. And many don't see the connection.

Her dad has given them all a gift. He loved her and sacrificed to be with her and didn't get his promotion at work. And that alone allowed him to stay home more…and his constant presence made her feel more loved and more normal.

And all of that has caused her to be a loving servant to many. Many think it is sad that her dad didn't get to fulfill what he could have...and they don't see the connection, either.

All of this could be the end of the blog, and you could see how important it was to see the connection between a mother and father's love and how it impacts a child and how that child impacts the people around them. But I want to tell you more.

I AM here in Megan's present, and I AM watching more of the connections way in the future.

(We're gonna travel fast through the future here, so pay attention and don't get lost.)

I watched Megan have her first son Daniel, and then I watched him listen to a lot of the same stories she heard from her mother. Daniel grew up and as a nineteen-year-old worked in a Starbucks, where on a Saturday in April in 2045, Daniel sat down with a fifteen-year-old and shared his faith in Me with that kid. That kid—his name is Nathan—had an interesting future. By the time his life was over, he had used his platform as a speaker to communicate to over thirty

that's right, Starbucks is still in business, but they look a lot different

million people. He communicated truth about Me that changed the world…in a way that I really like.

Here's the thought for you to consider.

People are put in your path almost every day.

Some are quite unobtrusive, and you might not even notice them.

Many are somewhat undesirable, and you don't *want* to notice them.

Some are right in your path, and you are forced to at least acknowledge their presence.

But

you make connections and the connections never die.

The thread just keeps unrolling through time—touching everyone, tying everyone together. It won't stop until you walk into eternity.

That's why…

EVERY

DAY

MATTERS.

EVERY

PERSON

MATTERS.

You have been placed in circumstances sometimes far beyond what you would have chosen and could imagine yourself in.

> *Be aware of those circumstances…they could be another chance to change the future of the universe.*

Look around.

Very near to you is a person through whom you can change the future of millions of people…

people whom you will never see…futures you will never know about…but I will.

And when we get together at My place soon, I will tell you all about them, and how your connection made the difference.

And you will smile with Me one of those everlasting, God-sized smiles.

7. BUBBLES TOO

April 12, 2007

Bubbles are thin layers of film made of liquid and soap that hold pockets of air. All the air inside the bubble is separated from all the rest of the air outside the film. Most of you know all that. As I mentioned in a previous post, it's pretty natural to want to burst a bubble when you see it.

There is one that I would like to burst. I have a strong desire for My children, the ones who love Me and claim Me as their father, to be who I made them to be and to relate well *in a culture that doesn't yet know Me.*

Some, however, have chosen to build a wall or a bubble around themselves to keep them away from the culture. They focus inward and tragically don't want outsiders in there with them. It seems kinda silly to Me when I see anger and rejection flare up inside your bubble because some of your artists decide to perform or write for the folks outside of your bubble.

Here is a thought…

Artists who are Christians have a better shot at changing the world than "Christian artists."

You now have your own Christian stores and books and singers and mints. You have created your own clothing and music and lingo, and you have isolated the rest of the world.

*You have built a bubble around yourselves and used insider thoughts to try to influence outsiders…**and they aren't getting it.*** As a matter of fact, they see your bubble and your actions inside that bubble and they hear your words and they are choosing to not get in there with you. And that is a wise choice. I didn't send My Son to die so you could form a club and dance at your own recital. I did it so all people could see Me and experience Me and understand forgiveness and grace and mercy and love, and so everyone would dance at My recital…and so I could dance at everyone else's.

The world has become dark, and bubbles can't be seen in the dark. Sometimes I want to take a God-sized pin and burst your bubbles

and hand you all a light instead.

Blogjot

I miss hearing the sound

of your voice

telling Me what you're thinking about.

9. DADS

I'M blogging today while I'M watching lots of dads raise their kids. Actually the blog isn't just for dads…it's for moms and dads alike, but toward the end of the blog I'll be doing one of those clever analogies where we look at Me being the dad and you being the kid, and since most of you picture Me as a father figure more than as a mom, hey…we'll keep it to you dads.

There are lots of you doing a good job and trying really hard. On your best days when you're not exhausted and pulled in a hundred directions…and when your head is clear and no one has pushed your buttons all day…
here is what you really want.

You want your kids to learn to live wisely.

You want them to be obedient.

You want them to know how

to treat other people.

You want them to respect life

and discover their gifts and use them

to the best of their abilities.

You want them to feel loved, and you want

to hold them when they feel rejected

and alone and like a failure.

You want them to learn to overcome

obstacles and get up and dust themselves

off and try again.

You want them to know all about kindness

and initiative, and discipline

and selflessness.

You want them to understand that success

isn't necessarily what they have

been taught by society.

You want them to help those

who are in need.

You want them to walk through life

honestly and with integrity so as to be

respected by those around them.

Of course, if you're like most loving fathers, a lot of things really **AREN'T SUCH A BIG DEAL.**

It really doesn't matter how far your kids can hit the ball or if they can hit it at all.

It doesn't matter whether your kids are more interested in science or sports history or cooking or law or preaching.

It doesn't matter if your kids' grade point average isn't perfect as long as they're studying and using their time wisely.

It doesn't matter whether your kids go to Harvard or even attend college—as long as they're celebrating and making the most of their unique giftedness.

It doesn't matter if they stay in your hometown or move around the world, or get a job making millions or live in a hut in Tanzania.

What most dads want for their kids (whether they realize it or not) is simply for them to be all that I have created them to be. Of course we all know that My definition of success and worth is usually different from the norm.

(BTW, all dads love to hear their kids talk great about their dad to others, and they love it when they hear "I love you, Dad," and when they get to look their kids in the eyes and talk and hug and laugh.)

So…here is that analogy I promised. You already are guessing part of it. But I've got a parallel for you to consider.

Catholics, Episcopals, Baptists, Methodists, Presbyterians, Nazarenes, non–church goers, Jews,

ALL OF YOU.

Hey!

Kids!

My Kids!

There are a bunch of things that really aren't that big of a deal to Me.

It doesn't matter much to Me whether you immerse or sprinkle.

I'M not concerned if you eat wafers or bread crumbs, or drink wine or grape juice.

You can wear jeans or shorts or a tux to church.

Not a big deal.

You can sing hymns or choruses or chant.

You can use King James or The Message or read from the original Hebrew if you want.

You can meet on Sundays or any other day.

You don't impress Me any more by being a preacher than you do by being a plumber or a nurse or a cook or a guy who goes from house to house every day spraying for bugs.

I don't love you any less if you are divorced than I would if you had been married for fifty years.

If you have made a million mistakes and done things you think I would never forgive...

Not that big of a deal.

I'M your Dad!

*I can't **not** love you.*

Here is what I want and desire most for you and from you.

That you discover Me and My love.

That you discover your giftedness so you can be all I want you to be.

That you are kind and obedient and humble and selfless.

That you know that I want to hold you when you feel like a failure or you feel alone or rejected.

That you see there are way too many things you think are a big deal, and in reality they are petty little things that separate you all way too much.

Oh yeah…and…being the Dad I AM…

I love it when I hear you tell others about Me.

And when you say *"Daddy, I love you."* **Wow**!

If you're a dad, you know how that makes your heart feel.

Imagine what it does to a God-sized heart.

10. TIME

I have given everyone on earth a gift. I might add that it is a pretty incredible gift. I have been watching lately what most people do with it. It makes Me sad and sometimes ticked off. I listened in on a few million conversations today and you were all talking about it.

Conversations went a lot like this.

"Gosh I just didn't have time."

"I wanted to, but time just slipped away."

"Sure wish I had more time to spend with My family."

"I didn't have enough time to get the job done."

Then there were phrases like,

"Sometime I need to…"

"Anytime you want."

"What time is it?"

"How many times do I have to tell you."

And then the one that really doesn't make sense at all:

"I sure wish I had more free time."

Here's a note: <u>There's no such thing as "free time"</u>!

This will sound a bit weird, but "time" is a gift I made for you so you could give it back to Me. The reason it isn't free is because for every second and minute and hour you use, you have to give something up.

You are trading time for something else.

Most of you wouldn't trade a thousand dollars for a dollar. Yet you trade time with your family for overtime at the office. You give up time to learn and grow and be with Me for time on your computers and your TV. You are sacrificing things that last forever for things that disappear quickly.

Forever is a long time.

How you use your time now

will determine, <u>however</u>,

what <u>forever</u> is like.

So you have in your portfolio the number of days, hours, minutes, and seconds you will be alive on your planet.

These are the gifts I have given you.

Every second counts.

Every day matters.

So every action, reaction, and transaction are of utmost importance…because

ALL TRANSACTIONS ARE FINAL.
YOU CAN'T GO BACK IN TIME.

Okay, I can, but you can't go back. That's why I AM God and you aren't.

It's time now. Time for you to think.

Time is like space. You can fill up the space you have and…you can run out of space.

The difference is, you can see when you are about to run out of space.

You could be out of time…really soon.

Make sure you fill it up with the right stuff before you run out.

Blogjot

I don't just want to be your God on Sundays.

I want to be your Father every day.

12. Expressions

One thing I made that I really like is human expression.

It goes along with feelings and emotions, and sometimes I see facial expressions that crack Me up even though I made them all.

Then there are things like gasps and oohs and ahhhs and exasperation sighs and sighs of contentment. All that just really makes Me smile—which is, of course, another great facial expression.

I watched some great expressions today. I watched as My Son started walking on water

on a lake,

in the middle of a storm.

But I saw the best expressions when I looked at the boys in the boat.

Their eyes got wide

and their jaws dropped

and their bodies got real tense.

I thought it was great that when they saw him walking on waves the size of their boat, they forgot to be scared for a second…they were too amazed at something they had never seen.

(It'd do a lot of you some good during some of your more frightening times to get distracted by Me so you could stop being so afraid.)

Anyway, the faces were delightful—especially when Peter decided to jump in. I wish you could have seen the faces of the other eleven.

But Peter's face—the determination when he actually made the choice to step out into…or on…the water. His eyes went from intention…to elation…to fear…and then when he realized that he was doing *something he shouldn't be able to do,*

his mouth got wide and his eyebrows went up almost to his hairline.

The veins on the side of his head were just about to pop as he went down face-first into the water.

Then Jesus reached out and grabbed him, and his facial expression of total relief was sheepish and magnificent. Jesus and I looked at each other and smiled.

We loved watching them. Every time Jesus did something like that, He would always pause for a second and look around just to see their faces. They had that astonished look for a long time after He fed the thousands with just a lunchbox full of food. They laughed and clapped and punched each other when He healed the lepers. They fell on the ground in amazement and cried and laughed all at the same time when He brought Lazarus out of the tomb. It wasn't laughing like "that was funny" laughing.

It was uncontrollable, *I-can't-believe-that-He-is-truth-God-and-we-get-to-be-part-of-this-and-my-heart-is-so-full-I-feel-like-I-can't-contain-it-all* kind of laughing.

I watched Jesus' face closely that day as well. <u>He had just cried</u>.

Then He looked at His friends with such intense love that it showed all over His face. Then with His brow furrowed and His teeth clenched He called Lazarus out. His own heart was beating as fast as it ever had, and then all of a sudden His tension released, and He looked around and saw the same faces I was watching…and He looked up at Me and out of the same eyes that just gave up those tears came a wink and a smile…

And I felt that had anyone been able to see Me right then, they would have caught a glimpse

of a brand-new expression…
just created on the face of God.

13. FAITH

I was back in the hospitals around the world today. Watching. People have faith in their doctors. They have faith in their anesthesiologist. They have **faith** in the teams of people working together who have done surgeries for years. But then I see their thoughts just before they go into surgery. So many of them start to wonder. Start to worry.

Will the anesthesia work?

Will I actually fall asleep before they start to cut?

Will I be able to communicate to them if I'm not out yet?

What if the doctor slips?

I know they have extra blood in case I lose some but what if it is the wrong type?

I know the rules and I know they triple check the blood type and there are plenty of checks and balances...but..what if?

FAITH.

It gets wiped away

BY *IMAGINATION*

BY *FEAR*

BY *EMOTION*

You have **knowledge** that seems to give you faith but there is something *spooky inside of you that washes all your faith away in times when you seem to really need it.*

Your faith in Me seems strong. Then all of a sudden you may find yourself being tempted to cheat or lie, to commit adultery, or to make some extra money in a not-so-honest way. Your emotions and imagination begin to take over and they over-ride your "faith" as they do in the operating room.

So then what is faith... especially if it leaves when it's supposed to get cranked up?

It is more than

knowledge of me...

more than

knowledge of my existence

and my omnipotence

It has to do with relationship.

It must be nurtured and grown.

Sometimes you have to go through the worst of life where you almost lose your faith in order for it to become real faith.

I understand when your faith wanes. After all, it was Me who built into you imagination and emotion. I know you struggle because you think I'M invisible and you can't reach out and touch Me.

But...

I'M HERE.

You aren't having to work on this thing alone. I'M working in you.

I'M your Father.
Your Daddy.

Most kids who are scared at night lose all their fear when their daddy comes into the room.
They've known him long enough and seen his love for them for a while, and they <u>know</u> and "feel" *that there is nothing to be afraid of.*

You may know about Me, but your faith is going to grow as we spend time together and you know you can trust Me.

As your faith grows, sometimes you'll start to wonder and ask all those scary questions.

And that's ok for a while,
but you should know the whole time one important thing...

Daddy's in the room.

14. GROW UP

I watch every day as millions of parents relate to their children in a myriad of ways.

One of the reasons I AM so intrigued by those relationships is that I want so badly for you adults to get a better grasp on our relationship. That is, the one between Me and you.

You see, *I AM your Father and you are My kids,*

and if you could grasp a bit better the picture of what being a parent should be like,

then you'd enjoy being a parent more yourself.

Let Me give you a few examples. I watched a number of parents today say the same thing to their kids. It's a phrase I'd like to erase from your heads.

In one instance a number of parents were in line with their children at a large amusement park. It was hot in Orlando, and most of the parents were sweating and close to their limit for the day. This particular line was for the Dumbo ride, and I could see inside the heads of many of the dads that this wasn't going to be their favorite amusement of the day. One guy wearing a shirt that said "**world's greatest dad**" was a bit afraid he might lose that title, along with his lunch, if the elephant went around too many times.

But it was the mom behind him who uttered the phrase I hear way too often.

She was struggling with two little twin daughters while having stood in the hot line for about forty-five minutes too long. The twins had gotten their second wind and grabbed their mom's hands and began to whirl around in circles spinning their mom into a frenzy.

They were making what were supposed to be elephant noises but sounded more like sounds you might hear from a cat if its tail were being run over. The exhausted mother had already spent most of her strength for the day, and what she had left vaporized as she spun helplessly out of control. Then came the phrase. ***"Girls! Grow up! Quit acting like children!"*** Her volume was loud enough to attract the attention of all the other parents standing in lines for about forty yards around. Most of them understood, and many of them had used those exact phrases sometime on their vacations. I knew the mom was tired, but something in Me wanted to put a phrase into the heads of the seven-year-old twins. Had I done it, you might have heard them say something like this: "Okay, Mom, you're right. Let's blow this lousy carnival stand and go get a beer."

Of course since I'M God, it wasn't in My nature to make that happen.

But it is in My nature to help parents know that they don't want their kids to grow up while they are still kids. If you rush kids to grow up fast, then there will be no need for roller coasters or Ferris wheels. Imagine telling Mickey to take a hike because you have outlawed childhood. You would close down your amusement parks, and toy stores would go out of business.

What do you think it means to grow up? Do you quit running and playing? Is an adult someone who quits making elephant noises and forgets how to have fun? Do you become adults when you quit playing games and start wearing suits and ties?

How mature is it really to wear a coat when it's ninety degrees outside or to tie something around your neck that cuts off the blood supply to your brain? Just to look proper? **What is that?**

Kids need to be allowed to be kids. You need to encourage them to experience life and people and laughter without appointments, schedules, and deadlines.

In another part of the same country, I watched a man in his late sixties crawling around on the ground with a stick in his hand. He was trying to get a little kid to look at something in a crack on the sidewalk. The kid had been standing near his dad and three other adults doing his best not to fidget or whine during the extremely boring adult conversation.

> *Whatever this strange man on his knees was doing, the chances had to be pretty good that it held more excitement than standing in the adult world of conversation.*

So he made his way over to see what this man was doing. A few of the adults stopped their conversation and watched. The older gentleman said to the kid "I want you to meet Herman. He'll be out in a minute." The kid waited for a minute, and the other adults began to wonder about the sanity of the older guy but then went back to their conversation. Finally the older gentleman called out, *"Quick, come here—he made it."* The kid ran back. The adults followed. An ant had come out of the sidewalk crack. The man introduced the boy to **"Herman the wonder ant."** And they watched it play on the stick and crawl to another ant called Wanda.

They were delightfully entertained for a while with this

tiny but wondrous part of My creation.

The "older gentleman" obviously still had some "child" in him.

He knew how to play and how to take the monotony out of life for a kid temporarily stuck in his dad's business world. He also happened to be the president of the New Orleans chamber of commerce. He had made it to adulthood without forgetting.

Too many of you grew up too fast. And you got your definition of adulthood all messed up.

You are parents now, and it's easy to get exasperated with your children because in many ways your worlds are different. (Believe Me…I know.)

But remember…

> **Don't let your kids grow up and forget that ants talk and children like to play… and no matter how old you get, you can still get down on your knees and introduce them to one another.**

Blogjot

FORGIVE

16. IN HIS IMAGE

I want to blog today about questions that almost all of you ask. I see them in your minds and I hear them in your prayers and I watch as you search in hundreds of ways for the answers.

"What am I here for?"

"What is My purpose in life?"

"WHO AM I?"

It's good to ask those questions. There are actually a few good answers that relate to all of you.

If you've read My Book, you know that you guys...all of you...were created in My image.

Okay...that's hard to figure out if you realize that I AM not physical. I AM bigger than the universe. I'M e v e r y w h e r e at once, and I know, see, and hear everything. None of you are like that at all. So let

Me give you a hint about what that "image" phrase really suggests.

Image is…

  a **representation**, a **reflection**, an **illustration**, a **likeness**.

  I'll go with representation and reflection on this one.

I created you to "represent" Me to one another.

                    To be a reflection of Me.

  I have more attributes than you can name, but let's start with…

Love

Acceptance

RESPECT

Light

Warmth

GRACE

TRUTH

LAUGHTER

Fun

Sensitivity

Consideration

Trust

Giver

Forgiver

EXCITEMENT

Adventure

Unique

Wonder

Words that describe part of Me. The part you can reflect.

You…a reflection of your Maker.

When the book says "in HIS image He created him"…it's really saying more about why than how.

To reflect.

That's WHY you were made.

That is what fulfills.

Those descriptions

↓

shining from Me

↓

bouncing off of you

↓

into the lives of others.

If it's happening, you're feeling okay today. Fulfilled. You're not asking the questions.

If it's not, you may not be feeling so well. And you're probably asking the questions.

It may be time to dust off the mirror.

BTW…reflections happen best when you are standing near to that which you want to reflect.

(That which you were made to reflect.)

17. LAUGHTER

I laugh a lot.

That may seem a bit weird to some of you. The picture of God in your mind isn't really very accurate, so it's difficult for you to actually imagine the Creator of the universe laughing.

But I do…and I love to see you laugh too. I put that thing in your brain that causes laughter, and it thrills Me when your soul is tickled and it sends a message to your brain and the sides of your mouth arc upward and your teeth show and your throat, chest, and gut all move together and…**LAUGHTER ERUPTS**.

Your scientists have created a word. It's big and strange and you may have to read it slowly to get the pronunciation right, but I kinda like it. It's called **psychoneuroimmunology**, the science of studying (among other things) the benefits of laughter to your immune system.

As they learn more about that, they are learning more about Me.

I put laughter in your system to make you stronger and healthier and happier, and it is, as I have said before, a great medicine that gives life. And postpones death.

I created **funny.**

I created **laughter.**

I created **the ideas behind funny words**

like...juxtaposition

and funny people

and I did it all for you.

> **LIFE'S TOO SHORT THERE ON EARTH TO TAKE EVERYTHING TOO SERIOUSLY.**

So…look around, lighten up.

I wanna see you **laugh**.

And when you do,

I'll be laughing with you.

18. GOTOYOURROOM ⟶▷ ▢

Today I decided to focus on parents of little kids.

I know that a lot of you wish I had written a parenting manual. Actually I did, but it just doesn't say "parenting" on it, and you have to use a bit of your own common sense to get how it all relates to parenting. It pleases Me a lot to see how so many of you figure out through all the trials exactly what you're supposed to do.

I especially like it when you start seeing your relationship with Me as an indicator of what your relationship with your kids should be.

I look at you and understand totally why you do what you do. You just haven't learned yet. You haven't grown yet to be what I know you will be. Certainly I AM often hurt and saddened, but I always know why you do what you do. **Because I see your future,** I know what the consequences and results of your actions and reactions will be. Much of what you are becoming is a direct result of the good you do, as well as the mistakes you make.

I know you wish you could see as I do while you try to raise your kids. But (just trust Me) there are things coming you don't want to know about.

Still, I have given you the manual.

You need to study it and then just trust Me as you follow it.

There is one thing a lot of you do that I think I might try. I heard about two million of you today say these words. "Okay young man, that's enough! **Go to your room!**"

Some of you said it differently, but all of you sent your kids to their rooms. Some of you did it because you thought that was punishment and they wouldn't like it. Some of you did it because you were afraid if they stayed around close you might lose it, so you sent them up there while you calmed down. Some of you just hoped that if they went to their room they would calm down and come back with a different attitude. Good thinking.

Here is My thought:

You worry and stress because you aren't sure how to parent. Your nerves are shot because you can't handle the schedule you have put yourselves on. You think things are supposed to be better than they are, and you put a lot of pressure on yourselves that doesn't have to be there. *You forget to follow My directions, and you forget that I love you and want to take a lot off your shoulders.* You become like your kids (in a bit of a different way), and you need something that will calm you down.

The thing you do that I'd like to do too is send My kids to their room. That is you!

I want to send you to your room. And you ought to stay there until I tell you to come out.

And now that you are older…I bet you would like it. Your room is the place where you can be alone and forget for a while all the stress of life and work. It's a place where you can rest. The problem is you usually don't show up there to rest until you're so tired that you just drop.

And here's another thing about your room that a lot of you forget: ⟵ I'M in there. ⟶

Of course I'M everywhere, but if you got sent to your room in the middle of the day and you weren't allowed to come out for a while, and you couldn't turn on the TV or the computer…you just might hear Me.

And you might stop and take a breath and relax and grab hold of some truth that would set you free.

Your lives are too full of too much stuff. Many of you have forgotten what it means to slow down…to be still and know that I AM God. So I'M going to go ahead and say it:

"Kids! Go to your room and stay there until your Father tells you that you can come out!"

(Enjoy!)

19. Evil

This is a warning blog. ☠

Too often people don't like to use the word "evil." When they do, they seem to think that it's easy to see. You often think of evil as those things you see on the news where people are killed or hurt. Some of you think it's lurking out there in the dark and because it looks scary you think you know how to stay away from it.

Here's your "think about this" moment:
Often, evil is beautiful and charming. It is alluring and draws you to it with such subtlety that you sometimes feel safe as you move toward it.

It draws you in…one unsuspecting step at a time. You make compromises…small ones…without noticing.

Eventually you are whittled down and captured…and suddenly it seems very dark…and you have no idea how to **escape**.

Oh yes, evil does its best work when you **don't** believe in it and when you **can't** see it.

Stay close to Me.

I AM light.

Bright lights shine so you can see where the shadows are.

Blogjot

I'd like to be part of all parts of your life.

Friendships

Finances

Health

Work

Marriage

Play

Dreams

Let's do all that stuff together.

I'll help you.

21. LIGHT

Entry date…very difficult to explain to you.

I AM existing here just before I created anything in your universe.

I AM also existing here simultaneously watching you there on earth in your time period.

As you have heard Me say more than once, I can be, and am, in all places at all times all at the same time. And of course I'M even outside of time. I know this is confusing to most of you, but I like the smile on some of your faces as your brain kicks into a gear that it forgets about periodically.

Just before I created the earth, there was *nothing*.

Nothing is a hard concept to get your head around.

Some of you are thinking that you have friends who totally have their head around nothing. ◁————

So there in the beginning I created light and darkness for your realm. The dark was called **night** and

See, God does have a sense of humor.

the light was called *day*. Back then…there wasn't fire, and I had yet to create Mr. Edison or give him some funky ideas about capturing electricity.

So when the clouds covered up the stars during the night, it was dark.

Like…really black dark.

No light whatsoever.

Then…later…of course, there was fire.

Then you did get your bulb and lamps and neon, and you learned how to turn your darkness into light, and you did it in some weird ways too.

Las Vegas…hmmm.

Some of you have had unexpected low-light anxiety when you've been sitting in your house or walking down the road and someone somewhere drilled into a power line fifty miles away and your city went dark.

Stumbling in the dark in a hurry…searching in the dark for a flashlight…hitting your shinbone on some chair you couldn't see and can't believe is there because you could have sworn it was in another part of the kitchen.

You swore anyway when the nerves in your shin sent the message to your brain that it had a problem.

> Darkness is scary sometimes.

So why a blog about dark and light?

If you've read any of My other stuff, you know that I AM referred to as **light** now and then.

I even refer to some of you as **the light of the world.**

It is written that *in Me there is no darkness.*

Here is what I want to say to you today.

I AM light.

When you know Me, you can see better.

How many of you are doing the same thing over and over, and you know those habits are what is causing your grief, your stress, your darkness?

How many of you are stumbling, hitting your shins and your hearts, and swearing because it hurts so much?

I AM the light.

When you know Me, you see better.

When you see better, ...

you don't get hurt as much.

22. LOVE LETTER

Sometimes as I blog to you, I feel what you might describe as anguish because I so much want you to know Me, yet I AM represented so poorly and incorrectly by so many. Too many preach about Me without understanding. They think I AM about rules and regulation. They think I AM mostly concerned about each good and bad thing you do and that somehow I AM way up on a throne somewhere keeping tally so I can show you your score and how good or bad you have been—and then dole out the punishment you deserve.

There are even churches who say they represent Me and yet when strangers come to your Sunday parties or your Bible studies or your revival meetings, they do not feel welcome.

Sometimes they feel just the opposite.

THAT IS NOT WHO I AM.

My Word is often used to make people feel guilty for not obeying the rules. I AM misquoted and misrepresented as people open up My Book and try to explain Me.

That Book is not so much a rule book as it is <u>a love story</u>. It's also an epic adventure with wonder and danger and rescues…and it starts at the beginning and goes to the end and the whole thing is about relationships and how much I love you.

So, this history book/adventure series/love letter starts…with Me creating you…to have a relationship with you.

I gave you everything and yet you wanted more.

That built a barrier between us, and I have spent the rest of history pursuing you so you could have the most significant life imaginable.

The whole story is filled with My showing you that the rules aren't as important as the relationship. It is filled with proof that it isn't wealth or fame or power that can fulfill you. The story shows that you are fulfilled only by a relationship with Me.

Too many people sit in too many churches hearing too many versions of the story that just aren't true.

If you are reading this and are one of those people who checked in at the church and checked out when you thought you heard the rules being read, then let Me ask you to check back in.

A lot of people do get it, and you will recognize them when you meet them.

When they explain the Book about Me, then you will see…it isn't about dos and don'ts.

It is indeed a love story that ties the beginning of the universe to the end of all days in a fabulous drama…*and you are one of the main characters.*

So if anyone or anything that had My name on it ever made you feel less than magnificent…

that wasn't real.

You are one of the main characters in the story because I made you and I love the way I did it and…

I can't get you outta My mind.

Love,

Your Creator and your Father.

23. MONEY

When I created the world, the first humans knew everything was Mine. Even though we've had trouble since just after the beginning, for a long time many of the humans were thankful that I would **share with them** most of the incredible things in this wonderful world I made.

As the human population grew and I let them become more independent, they had to learn how to get along and eat and grow and prosper, and they began to think that <u>they</u> were the ones who owned all that stuff.

They developed trade and commerce and made up words like ECONOMY and PROFIT and FINANCES. They <u>made more</u> stuff and <u>saw more</u> and <u>wanted more</u>…*and in the process they forgot the fact that all of it was Mine.* They didn't realize that everything was just on loan to them for a short while. So now there are whole towns and communities and neighborhoods full of people who have a lot and won't let it go because they think it's theirs. At the same time, millions in other parts of the world (*and even just in other parts of the same city*) have almost nothing, and those millions have no idea that other millions out there have the stuff I meant for everyone to share.

I've been thinking about setting up something on the planet to alleviate this problem.

We'd have to start all over again, but I could do that in a number of ways. *I've done it before—just ask Noah.*

It might be fun just to put everyone on pause for a bit like in that old *Twilight Zone* episode with the stopwatch. Only I'd be holding the stopwatch, so it wouldn't break with everyone frozen in time. I'd put everyone on pause, download some information into them, and then when they start up again they would understand that the following system is in place:

They all work for Me and know I AM the Boss and

own everything on the planet. Money is still in place, but they know at the end of the week the paycheck all goes to Me. They just hand the check over to Me. The economic system is still the same, so some people make millions more than others, but still they know it all goes to Me and that I have the option of doling out to each of them as much or as little as I please.

Imagine everyone's surprise and joy and excitement when they find out that I AM giving them nine out of every ten dollars they made for Me.

Most of them—I should say most of **you**—wouldn't believe My generosity. You'd be excited and you would actually want to know Me more and love Me more.

And the great thing would be that the other dollar would totally dissolve all world hunger and poverty and homelessness. It would educate millions and be used to cure disease and solve all the insurance problems and malpractice dilemmas. Talk about insurance reform!

And that is what would happen if this new system were instituted for just those who presently call Me their Father.

Oh, sure…

It'd be easier if everyone would just start using their resources *(**MY resources**)* wisely and giving back a small portion of what they earn,

But I AM not holding My breath on that one.

Hmmm…I really do like the idea of putting everyone on pause for a while though.

24. MUSIC

All of your sensory receptors are physically connected to "connectors" that send messages to your brain. These sensors tell your brain what your eyes are seeing, that your skin is **cold** or hot or that someone just *touched* you. Your nose lets your brain know if there is a barbecue place nearby, and your ears tell it which radio station button your fingers should push. Scientists and doctors have done a pretty good job of mapping what sensors are connected to what parts of your brain.

I put another set of connectors inside you. They connect your sensory receptors to your soul. These are invisible God receptors. When your eyes see a sunset, you feel something.

you can't see these

When your skin feels the touch of a lover, your pulse races and your throat gets tight. When your ears hear the voice of a long-lost friend, your heart leaps and your adrenaline kicks in. In all of these instances your soul is stirred, yet there are no physical connectors from these organs to your soul. It's kind of My wireless network I installed.

I'd like to focus on one of these for a few minutes.

One of My favorite gifts to you is the manipulation of sound as it enters your ears headed toward your soul.

MUSIC

I created it before your world ever existed. It R A N G through the cosmos and MAGNIFIED My wonder as angels sang out glory to their Father. It has continued to reflect Me and My love as you have used it through the ages to express all that is in you.

Today I watched and listened to music all over the earth. Throughout time.

I hear Paul singing in jail.

I hear slaves singing in the fields.

I hear Mozart when he was just seven playing wondrous melodies never before played.

I hear Billy on his harmonica, Jimi on guitar, Doc on his trumpet and Shanda on her berimbau.

I hear children in Africa blending their voices in a harmonious splendor that can make anyone anywhere smile.

Classical
  Jazz
    Rock 'n' roll
      Pop
        Rap
          R and B
            Blues
              Bluegrass
                Country western
              Chants
                Asian
                  African
                    Electronic
                  Folk
                    Latin
                      Opera
                      Regga
                      Hip-hop

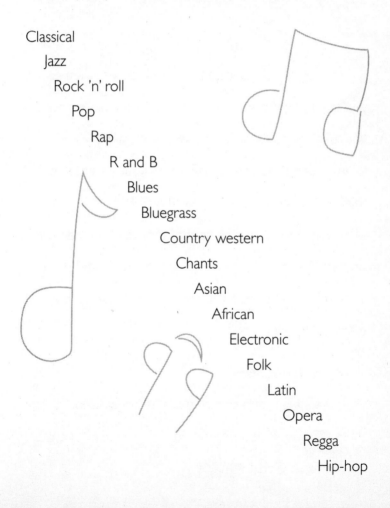

There's hundreds more. There is even the style no one can really name that finds itself in the shower of thousands of individuals who really can't carry a tune at all.

ALL OF YOU ARE CONNECTED TO ME
THROUGH THIS WONDERFUL GIFT
WHETHER YOU KNOW IT OR NOT.

And you're all connected to each other, whether you're playing the Autoharp for kids in a Bible school or you're in the subway looking very goth while your headset connects you to something your parents don't think should be labeled as music.

Music permeates the soul of every kind of person on earth. And you continue to create more and more styles, and it all is medicine for the soul…**even heavy metal and polka.**

A few notes here:

- It's a gift, and sometimes gifts are abused.

- Some of you make it your god instead of a gift from God. From Me.

- If it's being played in My house, and it's boring or bad, then you might have unwrapped a gift from someone else.

- I'M kinda glad you haven't combined country and classical too much yet. I'M not sure even I could handle one of Mozart's pieces put to words about trucks and trains and mama and beer.

The gift of Music is an expression for and from your soul…and your soul is connected to Me.

One of My greatest joys is when you
sing to Me and play for Me and worship
Me through the music I placed in you.

After watching and listening to so many of you do so much with this gift today, I want to pass along a message:

This gift
inside you
is a piece of
Me.

If it makes you want to move or dance, if it stirs your soul or calms your spirit, if it makes you wanna shout or run or...

makes you move faster on your treadmill while it is piped into your head through your iPod...

it's Me.

I AM the music.

Remember this: The next time you download a song from the Internet (legally, of course), or sing a song in the shower, or turn on the radio in your car to hear your favorite oldies, or slip on a pair of Bose noise-reduction headphones that you paid two hundred bucks for, and your favorite song comes ringing through your eardrums...

and your heart and soul become enthralled with sound...

and your mind is enveloped with this amazing thing called music—remember...

what you're hearing is a gift

from your Creator

because I love you

and I want to

stir your soul.

Blogjot

I know you get scared sometimes
of what you can't see...

Like right now.

No need.

I've got your back.

(And what's coming at you, too.)

26. OLYMPICS

The world was watching the Olympics this week. I watched you as you watched those marvelous athletes. Thousands of facial expressions went from **anxious expectation**, to *gasps* and **oohs and ahhs**, to frowns of discontentment as they watched Paul Hamm slip and almost fall right onto the judges.

Those who had hopes for him to win gave up hope for the moment. Those cheering for some of the other contestants

got more excited.

Then, *what seemed to be a miracle* started to take place.

Other contestants didn't meet their expectations, and Paul started to recover. By the time the contest was over, millions were amazed at the comeback of young Hamm. Excitement filled the airwaves and millions of homes as the National Anthem of America was played, and the gold medal was placed around his neck.

All of that was not what I was focused on.

I watched eleven-year-old Kyle Johnson as he watched the Olympics from his wheelchair in his living room and kept asking Me in his mind *why he wouldn't ever get the chance to do that.*

I also watched Kyle as a thirty-year-old today (it's a wondrous thing to be able to see your futures at the same time you are living in your present).

He was in a bookstore in Chicago, signing books for fans who stood in line for three blocks because they had read his incredible work that changed the way a culture thinks about life.

He was smiling and talking and laughing and *hadn't thought about the Olympics in over a decade.*

Sometimes while I watch people like Kyle and even his parents, I want to show them a picture of the future, but that really wouldn't allow the process they need to go through in order to experience Me the way they should.

So I choose instead to reach into their hearts when they let Me, and give them peace and grace that carries them through.

Some of you blog readers are a lot like Kyle was. You are watching others…wondering why you might never have a shot at their dreams.

Quit wondering.

There are new dreams you haven't had just yet…big dreams…dreams meant *just for you.* I know what they look like. And I know they can come true. After all, I can see your future.

It's right here in My hands.

One more thing.

Along the way, you will slip and fall…sometimes right into the judge's lap. And that will be good.

Because I'M the Judge.

27. TSUNAMIS

A lot of people ask a lot of questions about Me. Often when they can't get their questions answered sufficiently, they decide to put Me back on a shelf—*until they experience chaos or trauma in their lives,* in which case they forget about the answers they need and call out for Me and hope that I AM forgiving and loving and will forget about their aforementioned attitudes.

Actually I AM a lot like that...*I forgive and forget.*

I know there are a lot of questions that don't seem to have answers. Some of them you will understand as you mature and go through some struggles. Some you will never get. Some you will get just by human logic

(which, by the way, isn't always the same as divine logic).

When people ask why bad things happen, they often get their answer just by realizing that you can't have an "UP" without a "DOWN," a **front** without a **back,** light without **dark**—and you just can't have **good** without **bad.** We could go into that a lot further and talk about free will and how you have to be able to choose to love or you can't have love,

— but that isn't what this blog is about. —

I want to talk today to those people who really love Me and who are often the recipients of the hard questions. I've watched a lot of you lately. And when one particular question is posed, you either give a naive answer or a dumb one…or many of you have no answer at all, and you begin to wonder about Me yourself when you contemplate for a while.

I guess you're ready for the question now.

Earthquakes, tsunamis, floods, 9/11…

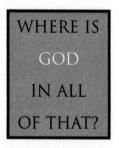

WHERE IS
GOD
IN ALL
OF THAT?

If He is a loving God, why would He let that happen?

I'M not going to give you an answer to this hard question. Actually, you're asking the wrong one. It shouldn't be, "**Why, God?**" or, "**Where were You, God?**" as much as it should be, "**Who are You, God?**"

But as I said, this blog isn't about answering the question.

I'M just going to tell you what I desire. Often when you know what I desire, the questions don't bother you as much.

My desire is for all of you to be with Me for eternity. You will live on earth for a little while first. The earth is *flawed*. So are the people who live there. That's why you'll only be there for a little while. You weren't even created for that to be your home… **it's just a stopping-off place.** My desire is for as many of you as possible to get to know Me and love Me and serve Me. To put Me above all else. One of the ways you do that is by serving others.

When buildings fall and tsunamis hit and
the flood waters take away life, My desire
is this—that those who know Me, serve.

- When the world is sending millions of dollars for
relief, then Christians should be sending billions.

- When the organizations of the world are sending
relief to countries who are devastated, My people
should be there in convoys…holding, helping, giving,
building, loving, feeding.

The world should see that when the natural course
of this flawed world causes chaos, the God of the
universe works through…

His people

and it is

His hands that are holding on to those who have
lost loved ones.

It is

His arms that are embracing those who need Him.

It is

His love that has brought them food and money
and water.

His heart hurts. And His people hurt…and they are
the first ones there to help and the last ones to leave.

An interesting thing happens when someone comes
alongside people going through trauma and walks with
them through the turmoil, and they experience love and
grace and help. Something changes. Ten years down the
road when they look back, the grief is still there, but it is
softer. What is still very strong and very vivid is the love
and strength and support that was given by others, and
the relationships developed and then continued. (The
trauma is never remembered or forged in minds nearly
as much as the good stuff…the God stuff.)

My desire is to use the hard things that come your
way to strengthen and solidify your character, faith, and

relationship with Me. Everyone will die. Everyone will suffer at times. My desire is to hold on to you and love you during all of your hard times.

Where am I in the midst of all the chaos?

> I AM RIGHT THERE IN THE MIDDLE. WORKING THROUGH MY PEOPLE, HELPING, LOVING, GUIDING, GIVING ALL THAT IS NEEDED.

My desire, however, is…that a whole lot more of you realize what you are on the planet for, and you allow your hands and feet and dollars and hugs and hopes to be Mine in someone else's life.

Here's another thing to contemplate. If everyone was doing what I hope for them to do, then millions of people all over the world would already be telling other millions about _Me_ and _My love_ and _My grace_ and what life was all about. And then of course that would create a big cycle of that happening all the time all over the place.

Then when the weird stuff happened (and don't get Me wrong here because I AM not trivializing this… when you hurt, so do I), here would be the result:

> There is another life after this one…some people get to go there sooner than they expected.
>
> For the survivors…if they let Me, they get to experience My grace and mercy in ways they never could have otherwise. Going through awful times together can make us grow closer, making the future much greater.

Here's something else for you to think about.

You see on the news the big events. You are aware of the earthquakes and floods and bombings. What you don't see is that many more thousands (than in any disaster that has happened) are dying every day of starvation and disease because they live in areas where they have no food and no knowledge of nutrition, no sanitation, no education. Compared to any disaster in the headlines, the numbers are staggering.

If you all would work together and look at this short time I have given you on your planet and decide what is really important, you could make a magnificent impact.

Interesting, isn't it?

Some people are asking of Me,

"*Where are You when disaster hits?*"

I'M ASKING YOU

THE SAME QUESTION.

28. NO ORDINARY PEOPLE

I want to blog today just to remind you about something.

> *I made everyone.*

<u>And</u>

I love <u>every single</u> *individual, eccentric, weird, selfish, greedy, loving, lying, wonderful, selfless, pushy, manipulative, whining, bragging, talented, lazy, serving, rich, poor, homeless, sick, influential,* last one of you.

I love them all so much that *I sent My Son to die for each one of them.*

Do you get this?

Nobody around you is a mere mortal. They were all created by Me…the Great Creator of All. They were created as spiritual beings. To live forever. <u>As My children.</u>

Okay…sure…they all, like you, ***do things that I don't like.***

But…

They all matter to Me!

A lot!

Now. Look around you. Think about your everyday life. Think about these people.

The people who work for you.

The people you work for or with.

The people who clean your house.

The people who do your dry cleaning.

The people who serve your food...at restaurants...

drive-throughs, doughnut shops.

Your spouse.

Your kids.

Your parents.

Your neighbors.

The seemingly invisible people all around you every day.

These are no ordinary people!

They are My children.

I created and formed them with tenderness and

love inside their mother's womb. As I said, they are not mere mortals! They were put on this earth by the Great Creator of the universe for a purpose, and they live with the breath of God inside them.

So…how are you treating them?

29. FORGIVENESS

I know some of you just read that last blog and started thinking about **how badly your boss treats you.** Some of you thought about how terrible you feel because of how you are treated by your dad or your ex-spouse and some of you even by your present spouse.

And your thoughts were, "Okay, I know You made them, God, *but how can I treat someone nicely who treats me so horribly…someone who abuses me so badly?"*

Seeing everyone as My children and My creation is the beginning of forgiveness.

I said something in another Book a long time ago and I know it doesn't make sense to some of you, but based on what I want you to understand, maybe I should say it again.

Love your enemies and pray for those who persecute you.

It doesn't seem to make sense, but trust Me, *it does a lot more for you than it does for your enemies*…and you _both_ need it.

I know how they treat you, and I don't like it. **I hate it, actually.** *But I want you to see them as I see them.*

The best way for Me to help you to see it is through your own children. When your children do things you don't like, or when they do things that you and they both know are wrong, you don't ever stop loving them, do you?

You just keep loving and praying for them…*because you can't not love them. They are your kids!*

*You need to see those who annoy you, who mistreat you, who get on your nerves…**as My children.***

Don't get Me wrong. I don't want you to be mistreated or hurt, nor do I want you to stay near those who might be putting you in danger. Lots of My kids need help, but they are still My children.

Together we will hate what they do to you. I will hold on to you during those times they treat you poorly, and I will listen as you talk to Me or pray to Me for them (your abusers…My children) and we both will love them…

    And it will be hard…but you see…I AM your father

    And they are My children

    And strange as it may sound

    That makes your boss…your brother

    And your wife…your sister

    And that will change everything if you let it.

    <u>It will change them</u>

    And

    <u>It will change you.</u>

Blogjot

You spend your life serving someone.

If it's you, you get rewarded with what you

have to give yourself.

If it's Me, I love giving all I have to

those who serve.
(I have a lot.)

31. POVERTY

I watched today as thousands of you responded to tragedy in the lives of those you love.

Accidents, disease, job loss, death…

Someone you know had their lives turned upside down.

You love them, and you are anxious to help in whatever way you can.

You find out there are needs that can be met, and it will help.

All it takes is some money, some energy, some initiative and sacrifice on your part and the loved one has a chance of being rescued or relieved.

All of you responded.

When it's personal, then to you, it is very real.

Sacrifice is easy.

Every day hundreds of thousands of My children are so poor they die of starvation and disease.

Millions are hungry and their lives are in danger and they desperately need help.

This pain is personal to Me. They are all My children. I AM their Father, just as I AM yours.

So the pain should be personal for you as well.

32. PRAYER

I love human beings. Today I listened to millions of them talk to Me. They use the word "pray."

Today 212 people in Keokuk, Iowa, prayed that

it would rain, while almost at the same time 124

people in the same town saw clouds and prayed that it wouldn't rain.

A lot of the prayers sounded like this:

> *"God, I just washed my car, so don't let those clouds break open. I've got a date tonight, and I want my car to look good."*

> *"God, we haven't had rain in weeks. My garden is dying. Could You just let it rain for an hour?"*

> *"God, my baseball team is on a winning streak, and I'm feeling good today. Those clouds look ominous, but if You could just hold the rain off 'til the sixth inning, well, that'd be great."*

"God, I am lying here sick in bed, and it's our last baseball game of the season. If it rains, we can postpone it 'til next week, and I can play. Please let it rain."

Meanwhile, a six-year-old in Keokuk was having a conversation with his dad about Christmas and trying to understand how long it would be until the day came. His dad tried to explain it by going through the seasons and explaining that when it started getting cold and snowy, it would almost be Christmas. Jeremy (the boy) didn't quite understand. So when his dad left, he looked up and said. *"God, would You let it get cold and snow tonight? Please? I really want Christmas to get here soon."*

I have to confess, even though it was the middle of July and 96 degrees in Keokuk that day, **I seriously considered intervening in time again and making it snow.**

But I never meant for prayer to be like a vending machine, or Santa Claus. You put your time in asking, and you **ask right** and HOLD YOUR MOUTH THE RIGHT WAY and *make your heart as open as you can* and MAKE PROMISES YOU PROBABLY WOULDN'T KEEP ANYWAY…and you wait for Me to come through for you. And then when I don't, you leave Me alone 'til the next test you didn't study for…or the next girl you hope pays attention to you…or the time you really hope you don't get caught, and you promise you'll never do it again.

That isn't prayer!

[Prayer is relationship.]

It's an ongoing conversation between you and Me— two people

who want to get to know each other better.

Sure, I don't mind you asking for things. Daddies like that. They just don't want to be all about responding to requests.

I want you to talk to Me about what you love and what you hate. I want you to thank Me for the things I do for you and ask Me what I want for you. I want you to forgive Me and hear Me when I forgive you.

When you don't get what you want, I understand your anger and frustration. But I want you to know Me well enough that you come to Me and say how angry you are. And you can hear Me say, "I know, and I love you. And even though you are angry now, I AM doing what is best for you because you are My child. I can't help but want the best for you."

I want your prayer times to be times when you sense My love   and   experience My joy.

I want to reach into the cell structure and electrical impulses going on in your incredible mind that I made for you, and I want you to walk away at times knowing exactly what it is I have said. And at times, I want you to walk away and have no idea what I have in mind for you. That way, you can trust Me and talk to Me all day and all week and all your life.

I don't want prayer to be just those times you get alone and spend a few minutes or a few hours. I wish for it to be **constant** in your life. I want you to feel and know that I AM walking with you every second. *And because I AM there, you can't help but notice and chat about almost every little thing that crosses your path.*

And there will be times, *because of who you are becoming* and because of who I AM, that you will go to your closet or your room or your bed, and you will cry out and I will answer. And My touch will make your insides shake and your heart pound and tears flow uncontrollably. And you will lie there in awe and be speechless because you *know* I AM there.

After you've experienced those times with Me, our relationship will never be the same. We will meet on a different plane, and we will walk, and we will talk, and your petitions will be fewer, and your praises will be greater. And it won't matter so much to you anymore that it rains or it doesn't…

and Christmas will be tomorrow every day.

33. PREACHERS

I want to talk about something that I

watch all the time and get frustrated with.

It happens every Sunday. Multitudes of people

go to what they call "church."

That is actually another frustration: that people call the place they

attend "the church." For the most part, it just isn't.

But when they get there, some of My most loyal

kids (as well as some kids who don't have a clue about

Me) stand up in front of their audience as

pastor/priest/speaker/bishop/leader, and they talk. They

talk about good stuff and true stuff, but for the most

part it is stuff that means absolutely nothing to the

people listening. *(I'M not talking here about those wild-eyed, stomping, yelling,*

self-glorifying bigots who get on TV and wear their thousand-dollar suits and make the

rest of the world scoff at the folks who humbly represent Me. That's another blog for

another day.) For this blog I'M just referring to the boring

folks who lead their people down the road of mediocrity.

And a lot of them use this weird voice. <u>They don't
even sound like themselves.</u> They have a different tone
and attitude and mannerisms. It's like they're bad actors
on a stage.

*I made them; I know what they're supposed to sound
like.*

*I wish they'd be more authentically who I made them
to be…that they'd be real and that the ones who aren't
gifted to speak effectively and honestly enough to engage
their audience would just sit down and let someone who
can accurately represent Me teach their people.*

*It's embarrassing when churches and people and the
media represent Me so poorly so often.*

When My Son was on earth, He said these words:

"I came that they may have life, and have it abundantly."

If people are asleep or bored or tuned out in an
audience on a Sunday, <u>that isn't life abundant.</u>

you didn't know I could be embarrassed, did you?

I AM joy

and life

and excitement

and emotion

and dance

and laughter

and relationship

and love

and imagination

and awe

and wonder

and drama.

I AM wild

and wonderful

and dangerous

and big

and hearty

and disturbing

and exhilarating

and My character and My truth set people free

from boredom

and sameness

and emptiness

and monotony

and tedium

and confusion!

I AM weary of people not knowing that about Me.

I AM sad watching people who are searching for an

abundant life step into boring buildings

(buildings with MY NAME ON THEM!),

hearing outdated music and listening to irrelevant

messages that misrepresent Me in a thousand ways.

I would rather those folks go to the lake where they

might get a better taste of who I AM.

Now that I have ranted a bit (which a God has a right to do—another one of the perks) I will say it is good that people are changing and some of you are getting it, and making things different. It is a delight to Me.

But for the rest of you, I'll paraphrase what a film director once said:

"Come on, people. I love ya, but ya gotta work with Me here."

Blogjot

I love you more than you love yourself.

I want you to be more fulfilled than you

want yourself to be.

And I know how to do that a lot better

than you do.

If you would let Me lead you,

you would be happier than you are

when you try to do it yourself.

Why don't you do that?

35. SNOW

Entry date 9-3-04

Today is December 21, 1987. I decided to enter into the
world and <u>DO SOMETHING KIND OF FUN TODAY.</u>

I made it snow in a small beach town in Florida.
Most of the folks there had never experienced that
before. Sure, many of them had gone off to the north
to see relatives, and some had gone west to ski. But a
large portion of this little town had actually never been
in snow before.

I loved watching their reactions.

It was great to see the children running around
catching snowflakes and screaming and laughing...*but
children do that with a lot of things.* What was delightful
was watching the adults, <u>the grown-ups.</u>

It's great to watch grown-ups forget to be grown up
for a while.

One particular incident caught My eye.

There is a bridge that goes over a bay separating
the mainland from the island in this town. The bridge

began to get very slick, and cars started sliding backwards, and people couldn't get across it. Cars were sideways, and some slid into the grass at the base of the bridge. **In almost every city in the north when this kind of thing happens, people get scared and nervous and anxious and mad.** They **yell** out their windows and often call My name out and add a few other words to it. But today, in this little town where most people had never seen snow, *something different happened.* It was a new experience. It was fresh. People weren't sure what to do at first. Then a young man got out of his sideways car and looked around at the other befuddled people who couldn't make their way over the bridge.

They all stood there for a minute (freezing in their short sleeves—that morning, when they went to work, it was sixty degrees outside), and then that young man reached down on the ground and scraped up enough white stuff off the grass to form a well-packed softball-sized snowball. **He smiled for a second** and then H U R L E D it at a complete stranger who was standing beside his car wondering how to get home. Missed by a foot. But when it splattered against his hood, it showered him with snow pellets. There were thirty-seven cars stalled on or below the bridge there today. And what happened next was wonderfully pleasing to all My senses.

All of those thirty-seven drivers (along with thirteen passengers) got involved in *one hilariously gigantic snowball extravaganza.*

These people didn't know they were supposed to be mad or frustrated. It had never snowed there before. It was **new** and **fresh** and **exciting** and **exhilarating**. And for just a few minutes, it changed their demeanor and their perspective on life.

> *It brought them joy and fun and life.*

I'M thinking about you the reader now.

You also have the power to bring joy and fun and life into the ordinary world of others.

WHY DON'T YOU MAKE IT SNOW FOR SOMEONE TODAY?

36. THE WRONG PICTURE

*I AM a little disturbed—**actually a lot disturbed**—that so many people and churches have painted such a distorted picture of Me throughout the centuries.*

People, of course, have no idea how to paint Me, but they have often attempted to paint the face of Jesus, and it intrigues Me that you almost never see him smiling or laughing.

Some have Me pegged as the CELESTIAL KILLJOY.

Lots of preachers and scholars have portrayed Me through their sermons and writings as one who is "set in His ways" and "scowls" at those things which do not go according to My heavenly plan.

This inaccurate presentation has caused many who listen or watch to place Me on a shelf with some of their other relics that have been collecting dust for a while.

I don't like being placed on a shelf. Especially before someone finds out who I really AM.

So if you've been listening to the wrong people or someone has handed you a picture of Me…before you decide to set it on a shelf somewhere, do Me a favor. Go read some of <u>My</u> stories.

Here are some of the things you'll see.

I once caused a donkey to talk out loud.

I had a big fish swallow a man and three days later spit him up unharmed.

I helped a few guys walk on top of water in a storm.

I made it nighttime in the middle of the day.

I set a bush on fire and kept it from burning.

Did the same asbestos kinda thing with three teenagers although I didn't start that fire.

I split the water of a huge lake right down the middle and held up the sides while over a million people walked on dry land to the other side.

Then I brought the water down on the bad guys who were following close behind.

Little bitty armies beat big ones. Sometimes with just instruments and pots and pans.

I made a storm stop and the waves settle with just a few words.

I took some spit and mud and used it to make a blind guy see.

Talked the leprosy right out of a couple of guys and made their ears and fingers grow back right in front of their amazed eyes.

I sent so many frogs and gnats and flies to a place one time that no one could see anything two feet in front of them.

I turned water into wine so a party would go better.

I set water and rocks on fire just to prove I'M Me to the ones who needed to know.

I fed over five thousand people with just what was in a kid's lunchbox.

And I watched a dead man hop out of his grave when I ask him to…mummy suit and all.

That's a short list. There weren't enough gigabytes in the computer to type out half of the long list.

(Did I mention that I also created the platypus, the giraffe, the kangaroo, and the grasshopper?)

Now do you still think I don't have a good time and laugh and smile? Do you catch a bit of creativity in some of My actions? Do you still want to put My picture on the shelf with all of the old relics you have collecting dust?

Like I said…those were just a few of the millions of fun things I've been up to.

I do small fun little things now and then too.

I helped some people find their keys today, and I made their car run when it was out of gas.

I've turned on television sets and turned off electricity just so some good stuff could happen to some good people.

Hey…I've even saved your life a few times, and you weren't even aware of the danger.

Okay…that's My blog.

Sure, I'M God so I'M old and Holy and Pure and Sacred. **But…***I'M fun and I smile and laugh and do exciting things that you couldn't imagine.*

> *So, tear up the old pictures you have of Me in your mind (or on that old church bulletin board). Quit listening to the folks who make Me look boring…and spend your time and energy discovering who I really AM.*

It's all written down.

Plus, you can see lots of Me in lots of people.

And…

I'M right here,

ready to chat.

37. DEATH

I watched today as many thousands of you

heard words that

— **changed your future.** —

The words struck a chord in your soul that you were never really ready to hear and there were thousands of different reactions. The words were spoken all over the world to every age and almost every race. They generally came from doctors who had just recently diagnosed your diseases. The doctors mouths opened and the words came out just like any other words verbalized that day or any day, but the power of those words changed your thoughts, your feelings, your actions from this day forward, your relationships…everything about you.

You found out you were going to die…

and that it will be sooner than you had ever anticipated.

Many of you had never anticipated it. *It's a bit strange that so many of you, although you know death is on everyone's calendar, have never contemplated that it is on your calendar as well.* Some of the folks who heard this news today will go into a deep depression; some will fight it; some will immediately begin to see how to control it; some will give total control over to others.

A few of you will do what you have been doing for years.

One of you wrote a song about what you would do, and for the most part, I really like it. The song speaks of a man who just got the same news. With that news he came to realize that his life on earth was about to end…so he changed.

Okay, he did a few things that I suppose are natural things to do for some. He went *skydiving*. He went *Rocky Mountain climbing*. He went *2.7 seconds on a bull named Fu Manchu*.

But then he grabbed hold of something better than a rip cord or a grappling hook or a bull rope. He grabbed on to the truth of what life and time are all about.

Here are some of his words…*which I couldn't have expressed much better Myself.*

I loved deeper.

I gave forgiveness I'd been denying.

I became a friend a friend would like to have.

I finally read the Good Book.

Of course the words flow better than that in the song…. I just gave a few highlights, and you can't put a tune on paper. *Actually I can, but that might scare you to death*

Many of you don't like country music, and you'll never hear that song.

But this blog isn't about that song. It's about **you** and **your life**…and **your death.**

Hey kids, listen up.

TOMORROW IS A GIFT.

But you don't have eternity to decide what you'll do with it…

and some of you won't even see tomorrow.

Some of you reading this will be gone by then. Some of you have six weeks, some have six years. And some of you have decades. But everybody has it on their calendar.

I mentioned time in a previous post. It belongs to Me, not to you. For those of you who have some left, here is your challenge.

Love deeper.

Speak sweeter.

Forgive.

Be a friend.

Get to know Me.

If you got to know Me like I want you to, you'd be overflowing with all of the above. And more than anything you'd be letting people know about this incredible Father you have and they'd see Me in you and they'd ask you about Me and you couldn't contain Me.

And that would be your **everyday, normal, walking-around-going-to-work, being-a-parent, being-a-sibling, being-a-human life** …and then someday when you sit in a doctor's office and you hear what to so many is sobering news…you might even smile.

Because you decided a long time ago to live like you were dying. And that included getting to know Me…and that means that you already know there is no such thing as death for you.

There is just moving from your house to Mine.

I'll see you soon.

Blogjot

Someone is needing

encouragements and **apologies**—

needing them like

air and **water**.

Close this book and call a friend.

39. WEDDINGS

Sept. 14, 2004

I watched a wedding today. Actually I watched about **thirteen thousand** weddings today, but I focused on one in particular.

I guess I need to talk about how that works before we go any further. *I can be outside of time and put Myself in it all at the same time*…or I should say all at once. I can see everybody all the time and I intervene as I please. When I say I focused on one, some of you might be disturbed that I might not have focused on the others. Most of what I say about stuff like this has to be interpreted metaphorically so you can understand. The way I made your brain and how you think is really not capable of getting the whole "time" and *watching-everyone-at-the-same-time concepts.*

BTW, I made your brain with that limitation so you could experience the wonderfully brilliant contrast that you will experience when you leave your short life and enter into the next one.

Don't get all disturbed about

HOW AND
WHERE AND
WHEN
<u>I AM</u>.

You'll get it sometime…except…I can't really say "sometime." You'll get it during another experience in another place in another dimension beyond this reality.

Okay, now back to the wedding.

The young bride was beautiful and the young man quite dashing (as are all My creations).

They held hands and indescribable feelings swept through their insides. He smiled a lot and did a pretty good job at holding back his tears.

She laughed out loud a few times—not on purpose, and not because anything funny happened. It's just the way I made her. Her nervousness caused it, and it held her together at a time when she could have fallen apart.

They said their vows.

They thought about their lives together, in sickness and in health, for richer and for poorer.

And they meant it. I know their hearts. I can see into their future.

I've already been there.

I AM there right now.

Health problems will come,

money situations will arise, and

they will be shaken.

They will complain and

they will doubt and

they will fight.

She will wonder sometimes if she should have done this.

He will wonder sometimes if there were someone more suited for him.

Sometimes they will forget the part in the ceremony where it was said that

they will build their marriage on Me.

Those times will be the hardest.

I will use everything at My disposal—

circumstances and

people and

books and

solitude and

tragedy and

laughter and

memories—

to nudge them toward an important truth.

There are things that she will do to hurt him every so often. There will be things he does sometimes that make her feel unimportant and unloved. And when they get quiet and reflective and…when they stop talking…

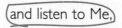

and listen to Me,

I'll remind them that they (along with everyone else on the planet)

do the same things to Me every day.

But I'M not going anywhere.

Sickness and health. Richer and poorer. I AM.

I'M going to keep on loving…and when My bride, My church, My people ignore Me for a long time…and don't speak to Me…and forget that I AM important…and when they do things that they know hurt Me…

I will not give up on them.

I will stand beside them holding their hand like the perfectly manicured groom in his elegant tuxedo, and even then, I will be saying *"To love and to cherish, to have and to hold from this day forward…till death brings us together…for the rest of eternity.*

40. GO OUTSIDE AND PLAY

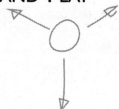

This will be My last blog for a while…at least for the book version.

BECAUSE…

I want you to quit reading and go outside and play.

That's right. **Go outside and play.** Some of you forgot what that was all about.

Your world has become so technologically exhilarating for so many of you that

YOU HAVE FORGOTTEN THE EXHILARATION
I PLACED JUST OUTSIDE YOUR DOORS.

When you were kids you found pleasure in playing in creeks and big yards and with dogs and ants, and if there were no man-made toys some of you made toys out of sticks and rocks. Some of you unfortunately lost your joy of the outdoors when your parents gave you too many warnings about the invisible dangers lurking beside you.

"Don't climb that tree, you'll fall and bust your head wide open."

"Don't throw those rocks, you'll hit something and then we'll have to pay for it."

"Don't run with that stick in your hand, if you fall you could poke your eye out!"

I've heard those phrases so much and so many times, I sometimes want to enter into the world just long enough to give some six-year-old the perfect reply,

> "Mommy, you really can't poke your eye out. You can poke it in further, but in order to poke it out you would have to stick something up your nose and pry."

I very much want children to be safe, but I also very much want them to savor the world of nature I have provided for them.

*I want them to **run** in grassy fields and **throw rocks** and **dive** into lakes and rivers and **lie** in pastures and **watch** clouds fly across the skies and **see** the shapes I have made and let their imaginations **wander** as they see dragons and puppies and alligators in those shapes. I want them to **breathe** fresh air and **absorb** sunshine and have rain **fall** on their faces. I want them to **laugh** and **have memories** of wonder associated with the nature that I gave them.*

And I want you…the adults…to have all that too.

But technology and appointments and schedules and cities and subways and smog and blogs and fear are keeping you inside huddled over your computers.

Your back is getting stiff and

your neck hurts and

your skin is pale and

you haven't breathed fresh air or

seen a dinosaur in a cloud

in twenty-one years.

So…this is the last official blog in the book

or on the site for now.

Because you have something better to do.

Go outside,

pick up a stick, and

RUN.

As *fast as you can.*

And…*don't be afraid because,*

hey,

you really can't poke your eye out.

EPIBLOG

Imagine this scenario. A man (or woman) goes into a bookstore and sees a book called

God's Blogs.

—Catchy name.

If the man is smart at all, he knows it can't be blogs because blogs aren't in books. They are <u>online.</u> But the name was catchy, so she buys it.

I'M switching genders at will in the story because I can...it's just a story.

He takes the book home and begins to read. Some of the blogs are weird and some are thought provoking. Some make his...her...your heart pound a little faster.

You are smart. You know it's not God talking to you in those words. It's just that <u>bizarre author.</u>

So what was that thing that stirred your soul?

Hey...it was Me!

I work through people and their words and their actions and their **smiles** and **touch** and **graphics** and **art** and **music**.

Truth is truth. The author of this book found some of it…and now and then put it together, and used it to set you free.

Those are words from My Book. ***"You will know the truth, and the truth will set you free."***

If he (the author) grabbed a few principles from the Bible, threw some personality on them, and wrapped 'em up in a paragraph full of truth…then those words actually were from Me to you…so you could be set free.

I AM your Father. Your Daddy. I want your life to be the best it can be. And I will do a million things to get your attention. That includes using bizarre creative-type authors to toss a little truth in your direction so you can get freed up.

Some of you haven't read much in My autobiography (the Bible).

You can capture a lot more of who I AM by going

back to that bookstore and picking one of those up. By the way, there are a number of versions of that. Be sure to get one that's a good read for you. It doesn't matter to Me which one you get, 'cuz like I said, Truth is truth…and it will set you free. All you gotta do is open up the pages.

I'll meet you in there.

HAPPILY EVER AFTER

This is the blog after the blogs. It didn't make it into the book so we sneaked it in to the back. It's weird.  *it really is*

Children's stories have been painting pictures in the heads of little ones for decades.

Almost all of you know them. You know the characters, the names, the villains, the good guys, and exactly what the trails through the woods and the ugly dragons and the dastardly wolves looked like.

At least in your heads.

But let's see what happens in the last blog in your book:

And so the princess

reached down and picked up the frog

and kissed him. The frog smiled and immediately turned into a wolf who devoured the princess.

That same wolf later was in the woods

watching a young girl with a red cape

and scarf who was on her way to her grandmother's house. He quickly got on MapQuest and found the cabin before little Red arrived. He locked Grandmother in the closet and coaxed the young girl near. However, he wasn't aware that Grandmother stored her **shotgun** in the closet and had served for years as Houdini's assistant. She easily untied her rope and came out of the closet blasting away.

All this commotion was too much for Red, so she opted to head on home on a different path through the woods. *She of course got lost* but fortunately happened upon a nice little cottage where it appeared no one was at home.

Red went in, tried some not-so-hot and not-so-cool soup and consequently decided to cook up some of her own.

Since she saw these five beans on the cabinet, she decided to fix herself a nice hot pan of bean soup. As soon as the beans hit the hot water, they grew into a stalk that climbed up through the roof of the house and on up through the clouds. She was very sleepy, so she decided she would climb the beanstalk to see if there might be a few beds she could try out and take a nap.

When she arrived at the top, she saw an older lady and inquired of her if there were some beds where she might lie down for a while. The lady smiled and said "Sure, but you look hungry. Here's an apple for you, and follow Me to the bedroom." Red wasn't aware that the apple was poisoned, but she had previously experienced insomnia problems so she was glad that the apple took the edge off and she dozed off to sleep.

The old lady didn't quite know what she was supposed to do next because she thought she was in the story with a handsome prince. She looked out the window expecting to possibly see him coming her way, but all she saw were clouds and a big castle.

Meanwhile three bears came home and saw the giant stalk going through their roof, and they were so mad they almost went through the roof themselves. Just then seven little dwarfs came rushing in asking what the heck the bears were doing in their house. Because they had not taken their meds they were a bit disoriented but soon got their bearings and apologized and decided to head on over next door to their own house.

However, as they left the bears' cabin, they spied the large stalk growing up through the clouds. "Why not climb that beanstalk?" they exclaimed together. It would be an adventure, and after all, most every day of their lives had just been boring—getting up and then off to work…every single day! This beanstalk would give them a great break, they agreed.

Meanwhile, back at Grandma's house, it appeared that the wolf had only been wounded, and as he was waking up he realized that the original spell cast upon him to make him a frog went haywire somehow, but he was finally turning into the prince he once was. When Grandma saw this, although she was a bit attracted to him herself, she told him he'd better hurry and go find Red. She knew her granddaughter would like this wolf-turned-prince.

The wolf-prince took off out the door and of course headed down the wrong path. He ran into another wolf that looked a lot like he had looked just hours ago, but this wolf could talk and he seemed to be after some pigs. A couple of houses had already been destroyed and he was blowing as hard as he could trying to knock down a brick house. The prince (formerly known as Wolf, formerly known as Frog) thought this was interesting and decided to just let him stay there and blow 'til he hyperventilated. He ignored the other wolf as he headed on down the path to find Red, who he *knew* would be in trouble by this point.

Meanwhile up in the sky above the stalk…the old lady had made it to the castle and ran into a humungous giant saying some kind of silly rhyme about bones and bread.

When the giant saw the old lady, he asked what she was doing, and she mentioned she was hungry but all she had at home were bad apples. She also inquired about what story she was in because she thought there was supposed to be a prince in this one. The giant was frustrated because he heard there was supposed to be a kid named Jack in his story, so the two of them chatted for a while.

When they got to talking, she found out they had been to the same fancy ball a number of years ago and just didn't recognize each other. He disappeared for a minute and came back with a little glass slipper about the size of his pinky finger. He handed it to her and she gasped. As she tried it on, **of course it fit perfectly.**

They stared at each other for a minute when all of a sudden the seven dwarfs came in. Actually only six of them (Sleepy had gotten tired and found a bed in a little house near the top of the stalk).

The dwarfs demanded to know where their friend Cinderella was. The old lady was so happy about the new relationship with the giant that she didn't care much what happened outside the castle, so she told them about Red and the apple and how there was a spell on her that couldn't be broken until a handsome prince kissed her. Since the dwarfs had no idea where Cindy was, and because they didn't want to go back to work, they decided to make the most of their little adventure atop the stalk and try to find a prince to kiss little Red.

Meanwhile down on the ground the former frog-wolf-prince had finally come to the cabin with the pot of soup on the stove and the stalk going from there up through the roof. He was afraid Red was up there, but he was also afraid of heights, so he thought and he thought, and finally he came up with a plan.

Minutes later, he found the non-prince, now hyperventilated wolf sitting near the brick house, trying to come up with a new plan of his own. The prince wolf offered the out-of-breath wolf gingerbread cookies and porridge if he would come help him blow down the beanstalk.

Well, together they huffed and puffed and sure enough…the beanstalk came down.

This was a real problem for the dwarfs and little sleeping Red, all of whom were now stuck up in the air with no stalk to climb down.

There seemed to be no way for them to get back to the ground. Then they realized, hey…if the writer of this story could change things around like he had been doing during this whole story, then surely they could ask him to type in a few paragraphs that could get them back where they belonged!

They reminded him that he had yet to mention the **cow.** So sure enough, when the cow jumped over the moon, they were all ready, and on her way down they jumped on her back, and even though it was a pretty hard landing, they all made it.

Actually the blow against the ground caused little Red to wake up, so she didn't need the kiss of a prince. She was a bit young for kissing anyway, and she had heard that you could get germs. Besides, she just wanted to go home.

Of course this left the former frog-wolf-prince standing there with a blowhard wolf whom he really wasn't that fond of. He knew the story was almost over, and sadly he realized that during the whole time he had not really accomplished anything worthwhile to speak of. So he decided to be proactive in making some adventure happen before the story ended.

The prince explained to the wolf that if he would get out of this story and go back to Grandma's house, he would need to put her in a different closet and use duct tape. And he was sure Red would come by again soon.

He then knocked on the door of the brick house and chatted with the three pigs and ended up inviting them to a barbecue.

The dwarfs eventually had to go back to work. All but Sleepy. **No one was sure exactly where he was.**

The three bears stayed inside their house for the whole winter and no one ever came to see them. Probably because the author got this story into the hands of Goldilocks and she was so scared she just stayed in and ordered pizza and Chinese.

Meanwhile the original spell wore off the former frog-turned-wolf-turned-prince, and at the barbecue he turned back into a frog again, but he didn't really care because living in a pond swimming around all day and catching flies with a very long and flexible tongue was…**well, it just kind of made him happy**.

Later that week little Red went to see her grand-mother only to find her grandmom had moved because she found this giant of a man who had her slipper and she was never coming back to the little cabin again.

The wolf, who had been waiting there for both Grandma and Red, got tired of waiting and heard about the barbecue and that the pigs were gonna be there. He meandered over thinking he might catch them out of their brick house. But he didn't see them, so he just sat down and had a feast while the dwarfs worked overtime bringing him his all-you-can-eat pork and beans.

~~The end~~

What in the world kind of blog is that?

I told you it would be different. Surely it's way too weird to glean any kind of life-changing truth from.

Unless you consider this.

We've all heard stories that sound familiar where we think we know what happened and how it all will end. That's not true in real life.

Sometimes your stories will go in directions you couldn't imagine.

Your life will take some turns and twists that will throw you way off course.

Sometimes it will seem catastrophic.

But if you know Me, <u>your Storymaker</u>…you can handle what comes your way no matter how strange or how hard it might get.

You should know too, that one day you will get to what seems like the end of the story. But then you will turn the page and find out that the story you were in was just chapter one.

Your Storymaker has written an amazing never-

ending story that gets started right after "the end."

And…

you and I live

happily

ever

afterlife.

THANK YOU

This is the page where people normally thank people. It's kinda weird because in most of this book I am speaking in first person as God...so I was contemplating...if God were thanking people, who would that be? He couldn't really thank Adam or Eve or any of the rest of us who really mess things up, even though our mess-ups help us see His grace and mercy and wonder and love. The only person He really could thank would be...God...Himself. Normally, in human terms, that might seem selfish.

Here is a cool thought.

When God is selfish, meaning He puts Himself first, He is really being totally selfless. The highest, most holy thing anyone can do is to hold Him up and glorify and honor Him. Whenever anyone does that, it is great for all humanity. Which of course means that if God does that, it is good for us. So if I were speaking for God in this thank-you page...I would say, "Thank God."

But here I am actually speaking for me and not Him. And I first want to say, Thank God. I would never presume that I could actually speak for You, but thank You for letting me try to take Your words and principles and express them the best way I know how. My desire is that You use this book for Your glory.

And now to thanking people:

Bob Jones (not the guy the university was named after), my history professor who stood in front of the class my first day in college and said, *"Just because someone stands in front of you as an authority, doesn't mean they are correct. And just because you read it in a book, it isn't necessarily true."* That made me question my parents, my preachers, and the Bible for the first time in my life. Which helped me to find out they were right all along. But now my faith is mine and not theirs.

Janet McReynolds. Philosophy professor. Met her the same day I met Mr. Jones.

First atheist I ever met. She helped me discover even more about how real God was.

Harvey Fisher who pulled me off my bike and beat me up when I was in fifth grade.

Somehow I'm sure that must have helped me.

Bill Webb. You may not know it, but you set the standard for youth workers back in 1970.

Joe Pierce. The first preacher I ever met who was a normal guy. Thanks for sitting at the table late at night and talking about life and carrier pigeons.

Ralph Holowinski. (I have no idea if that's how he spelled his name.) I only met you twice. But thanks for talking me into selling books in Pennsylvania for a summer.

Joe Pierce Jr. Thanks for going with me to Pennsylvania that summer.

Richard Howe. I haven't seen you or heard from you in sixteen years. We have some conversations to finish. Call me.

Grady Nutt. I know you are in heaven now, so if God happens to share book stuff from down here up there, your advice and your example got me a long way.

Mike Yaconelli. I expect you are still jumpin' around shouting woo-hoo even though you've already been in heaven for just over a year. Your courage to get out of the church-box helped a lot of us see to lose our religion and gain a relationship.

Susan. Thanks for getting me to the right doctor. I know God told you what to do.

Dr. Kassabian. Thanks for being a good surgeon and removing the correct organs and sewing me up without leaving anything behind. God still wants to do more stuff in you.

andy stanley

reggie joiner

louie giglio

Andy, thanks for doing what God has given you to do. That has allowed me to do the same.

Reggie, thanks for thinking out loud. Louie, thanks for painting pictures of God on the BigStuf canvas.

The BigStuf staff and family. Wow! Can you believe it?

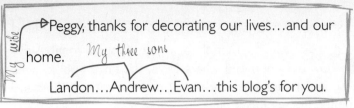

Peggy, thanks for decorating our lives…and our home. *My wife*

My three sons

Landon…Andrew…Evan…this blog's for you.

Let's see…there's Steve James, John Woodall, Boyd Bailey, David Wills, Mike Kendrick, Joel Manby, Brad Sitton, Woody Faulk, Ron Stanley, Bobby Cannechio, Duffy Robbins…Brian, Jamie, Sheila, Megan…hmmm…Mike and Betty Womack, Paula Nelson, Jeff Holley, John Williams, John Turner, Brian Coley, Greg Payne, Hadley Brandt…gosh…

Ok…now it's really frustrating because when you stop to think about it, everybody you know, whether you like them or not, pretty much helped create who you are…and how you think…and what your write…so thanks everybody.

Thanks to the folks at Multnomah (sounds like a *laxative*) for letting me do this thing out of the normal publishing box.

This is where publishers usually put a heading called "About the Author." Then they list my vocation, family stats, maybe how old I am, and where I live. But since I get to write this I thought it'd be a good idea to just start writing stuff instead of handing in my official bio.

Mom and Dad named me Lanny, after some Broadway pianist. I think they hoped I would play the piano wonderfully for them someday. I tried. Never could get my right and left hands to do different things on the keyboard.

This is me at nine months.

Across the page is me fifty-one years later.

In between those two snapshots I hung out in the Midwest playing baseball and basketball, going to college, being Schroeder in *You're a Good Man, Charlie Brown* (where it appeared as though I could play the piano like Lanny Ross). I went to church every Sunday and thought I knew God. Then I started having professors tell me God wasn't real, and I started watching a lot of family members and friends get sick and die, so I decided God may actually not be who I thought He was (if He was).

A long search, a lot of reading, a lot of chatting with a lot of different kinds of people and a lot of God showing up in weird places in life...helped me to actually know Him better and know that He was...is....and always will be. And He loves me a lot.

So I ended up in my twenties in Panama City Beach, Florida, working for a church where I thought I knew God. I hung out with a bunch of teenagers for a bunch of years and revealed to them all the secrets of the universe. I quit that church after nine years and traveled around the country until I met Peggy Anderson, who told me I should marry her...so I did. We built ourselves a little beach house and had some kids (great ones...three boys) and moved to Atlanta, Georgia, so I could help my good friend Andy Stanley start a little church.

God seemed to be all over that. Then we started doing big camps for teens in Florida and God seemed to be all over that. Life was good.

Then I got cancer. God seemed to disappear. Over the next few years in the midst of facing my greatest fears, I got a fresh, wonderful, exhilarating glimpse of God. He was different than I had thought before.

So now, I would say I know God. And I am sure that I will probably rediscover Him again and again as long as I live and...after that.

This book is my attempt to share with you a bit of the glimpse that I have had of Him lately. I hope you see what I see.

By the way...the next page should give you a hint at what my real vocation is. It's pretty fun. Check it out. ⟶

Lanny Donoho...your friendly neighborhood author of this book is also the Head Honcho of the infamous organizations called: **Big Stuf Camps and Big Stuf Productions!**

Since we can use the whole page here, let me say that again a bit bigger.

Big Stuf Camps
Check 'em out at
www.bigstuf.com

If you know of a youth group from a church that does the camp thing in the summer...send their leader that link and tell him or her...hey, you gotta take your youth group to these. Fifteen hundred kids a week on the world's most beautiful beaches of Panama City Beach, Florida. Most creative, engaging, fun, God-centered, life-changing events in the country.

Or...if you wanna communicate with the author about anything worthwhile...go to

www.godsblogs.org

Big Stuf Camps

Bigstuf was organized in 1988 (a.k.a. Youth Ministry Resources). We have been working on getting organized ever since. We are a nondenominational, nonprofit ministry based in Alpharetta, GA.

Our Mission

...is to creatively communicate the refreshing Spirit of Christ, the truth of His word, and the difference living for Him can make in our lives.

Our Desire

...is to create environments that enhance the opportunities to lead students into a growing relationship with Jesus Christ. All of the elements and logistics of our events are geared to that end. The people who lead our camps are balanced, gifted people who have a history of character and integrity.

Big Stuf Productions

Our Mission

...as we assist other organizations is to honor God by developing relationships and doing business with integrity, honesty, and excellence.

Consulting, sales, and rentals:

• Eiki • Dalite • Pink Inc. • Truss • Drape • Digital Juice • Aluna Blue • Artbeats •

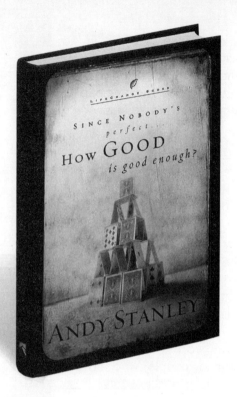

How Good is Good Enough?

by Andy Stanley

Goodness is not even a requirement to enter God's kingdom—thankfully, because we'll never be good enough. And Christianity is beyond fair—it's merciful.

1-59052-274-5

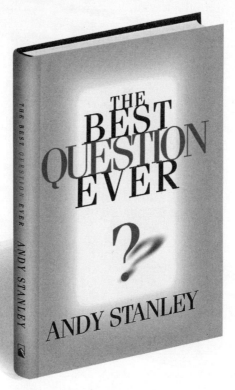

Best Question Ever

by Andy Stanley

Tired of living with regrets? Here's a revolutionary way to make decisions—in the form of one, simple, life-changing question.

1-59052-390-3

Up to You

It's Your Life, Choose Wisely
by Andy Stanley with Heath Bennett

Decisions, decisions. Life is full of 'em. Now, by
asking just one simple question, you'll make the best
one every time—with confidence. Guarantee yourself
a regretless future!

1-59052-516-7

Am I Good Enough?

Preparing for Life's Final Exam
by Andy Stanley

In this updated edition of the bestselling book,
teen readers find out why Jesus taught that
goodness is not even a requirement to enter
heaven—and why Christianity is beyond fair.

1-59052-467-5

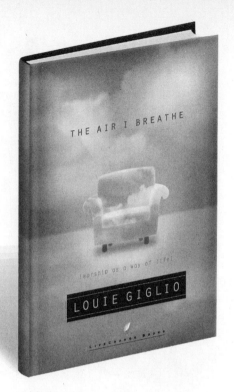

The Air I Breathe

Worship as a Way of Life
by Louie Giglio

As a species, we are deeply religious, serving with
abandon the things we have declared worthy. It's not
something we're taught at church. We arrive from the
womb ready to worship. However, to worship anything
less than God robs both Him and us.

1-59052-153-6

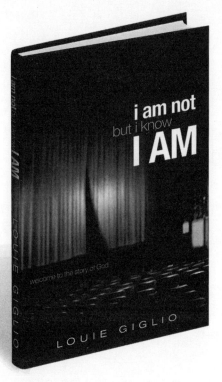

I Am Not But I Know I Am

Welcome to the Story of God
by Louie Giglio

Find freedom from the worries that strangle you—
get to know the God who is everything you aren't!

1-59052-275-3